pasta

pasta

Silvana Franco and Lindy Wildsmith

with photography by Nicki Dowey
and William Lingwood

RYLAND
PETERS
& SMALL
LONDON NEW YORK

Senior Designer Toni Kay
Senior Editor Clare Double
Production Toby Marshall
Picture Research Emily Westlake
Art Director Leslie Harrington
Publishing Director Alison Starling

Food Stylists Silvana Franco, Lucy McKelvie
Stylists Helen Trent, Antonia Gaunt

First published in Great Britain in 2008
Ryland Peters & Small
20–21 Jockey's Fields
London WC1R 4BW
www.rylandpeters.com
10 9 8 7 6 5 4 3 2 1

The recipes in this book were first published in *Pasta* and *Pasta Sauces*, also published by Ryland Peters & Small.

ISBN: 978-1-84597-758-0

A CIP catalogue record for this book is available from the British Library.

Printed in China

Notes

• All spoon measurements are level unless otherwise noted.

• Eggs are medium unless otherwise specified. Partly cooked eggs should not be served to the very old, frail, young children, pregnant women or those with compromised immune systems.

contents

introduction

For those of us who lead busy lives but still want to eat healthy, fresh food, pasta is often the first choice. It's one of the few dishes that can be ready to eat within half an hour of getting home, and it's also a guaranteed hit with guests. Many sauces, particularly meat ones, can be prepared in advance, making life even easier, especially when having friends over. Meat sauces also freeze well, so you can make a double quantity and freeze half.

Pasta makes ideal everyday food, because it can be incredibly varied. Pasta goes with meat, seafood, vegetables, cheese – the list is endless. In this book you'll find a fantastic range of sauces, all using readily available ingredients and some only requiring what you'll have in the cupboard.

The recipes use dried pasta, except when you're creating stuffed shapes. Making your own pasta is surprisingly easy and satisfying – and it will never fail to impress! For everything else, go for good-quality, Italian-made, dried egg pasta, or that made with 100 per cent durum wheat. It comes in a huge range of shapes and sizes. If you need help deciding what to buy, see page 8 for tips on which pasta to serve with which sauce.

Pasta is easily adaptable too – don't be afraid to experiment with the recipes. If you want to avoid dairy produce, try adding chopped herbs or nuts, or breadcrumbs fried with garlic and herbs, instead of Parmesan cheese. For vegetarians, the choice is huge. Many recipes that include meat added to a sauce based on vegetables or cheese can be adapted by substituting ingredients such as sun-dried tomatoes, capers, olives and nuts for the meat. Fish eaters could add smoked fish and anchovies.

Pasta may be quick and easy to prepare, but it should still feel like a welcome treat. Dress your pasta as you would a salad and take plenty of time over it. Add lots of Parmesan, herbs, olive oil and other seasoning before serving, and put an extra dish of Parmesan on the table, too.

dried pasta

There's a huge selection of dried pasta shapes, sizes and lengths available. They can be divided into basic categories of strands, ribbons, tubes and shapes. Your choice will largely depend on the type of sauce you are serving. Strands (such as spaghetti) and ribbons (such as fettuccine) are ideal paired with fine and oil-based sauces, which coat the lengths evenly. Tubes (such as penne) or shapes (such as conchiglie) go well with chunky or meaty sauces, as they nestle together in the bowl and catch the sauce inside their shapes. However, these are just guidelines – there will always be exceptions. Choose pairings that you like or that suit your mood.

STRANDS AND RIBBONS

Long pasta comes either as long strands (hollow or solid) or as flat ribbons ('fettucce').

Strands: Spaghetti, spaghettini, bucatini (these are all hollow).
Ribbons: Tagliatelle, linguine, tagliolini, fettuccine, pappardelle.

TUBES AND SHAPES

Tubes and shapes are either plain or ridged – 'rigati'. The ridges help the sauce cling to the pasta.

Tubes: Penne, chifferi, rigatoni, macaroni or maccheroni.
Shapes: Fusilli, conchiglie, farfalle, orecchiette, gemelli.

PASTA FOR SOUPS

Very small shapes are ideal for soups, as they look very pretty and delicate and don't dominate the soup.

Soup pasta: Anellini, fedelini, stelline, alfabetini, ditali.

PASTA FOR BAKING

Lasagne are flat sheets of pasta, layered with sauce in baked dishes.

Cannelloni are large tubes for stuffing and baking.

FLAVOURED PASTA

Pasta flavoured and coloured with spinach, tomato or squid ink are the most common types, although beetroot, basil and saffron flavours are also available.

COOKING DRIED PASTA

• Allow 75–125 g dried pasta per person, depending on how substantial the sauce is and, of course, on appetites.

• Cook pasta in a large saucepan with plenty of salted, boiling water, at least 4 litres per 500 g pasta. Don't skimp on the salt, or the pasta will taste bland – add it to the water just before you add the pasta.

• Add the pasta to the boiling water all at once.

• Keep the water boiling and cook with the lid off. Stir with a wooden fork to stop it sticking, but don't add oil to the water: it's a waste of oil.

• Don't overdrain and never rinse cooked pasta – the coat of starch helps the sauce cling. Reserve a cup of pasta cooking water before you drain, then add it to the sauce if it seems dry.

• Cook until al dente, literally 'to the tooth', testing often by removing a strand or shape and tasting it. Al dente pasta is springy – when it is overcooked it is flabby and when undercooked has a chalky centre.

• Don't delay – pasta gets cold quickly. Return drained pasta to the warm pan or to a warmed serving bowl, add the sauce, toss with a fork and spoon, then serve.

PARMESAN – YES OR NO?

Generally, yes. Pass a small block of Parmesan and a fine grater around the table so everyone can grate their own. The only time Parmesan should not be offered is if the sauce is fish or seafood. It just doesn't go, and you would certainly never see it on an Italian table. That said, if the seafood or fish sauce is creamy, for some reason a grating of Parmesan can be more than welcome. Pecorino, also a hard cheese but made from sheep's milk, has a tangy flavour and can be a good alternative to Parmesan.

fresh pasta

There's something really satisfying about making pasta at home. It's quick using a food processor and pasta machine, but you can easily make and roll the dough by hand. If you can't find Italian tipo 00 flour, opt for a strong bread flour. Eggs add richness and colour and make the dough softer and easier to work.

300 g pasta flour, such as tipo 00, plus extra for kneading and rolling

a pinch of salt

3 small eggs

makes 500 g

Put the flour and salt in a food processor, then add the eggs. Process in short bursts until the mixture forms sticky crumbs. Alternatively, sieve the flour into a bowl, sprinkle with salt and make a well in the middle. Add the eggs to the well and, using your hands, gradually work the flour into the eggs, using circular motions.

Transfer the mixture to a lightly floured surface and bring together with your hands to form a soft dough.

Knead the dough for about 5 minutes, until it feels smooth, then wrap in clingfilm and chill for about 30 minutes, but for no more than 1 hour. Chilling is essential, and will make the dough easier to roll and less likely to tear.

Divide the pasta into 4 pieces and roll each piece through a pasta machine, going down a setting each time and dusting with flour when necessary, up to and including the thinnest setting. If you don't have a pasta machine, roll out the dough with a rolling pin on a lightly floured surface to about 2–3 mm.

Note If the pasta is to be filled, use each sheet immediately after rolling, or the pasta will start to dry out and crack when handled. If you are making plain ribbons, strands or shapes, leave the sheets of dough to dry on a clean tea towel for about 30 minutes before cutting. They can be left to dry out for up to 2 days before cooking.

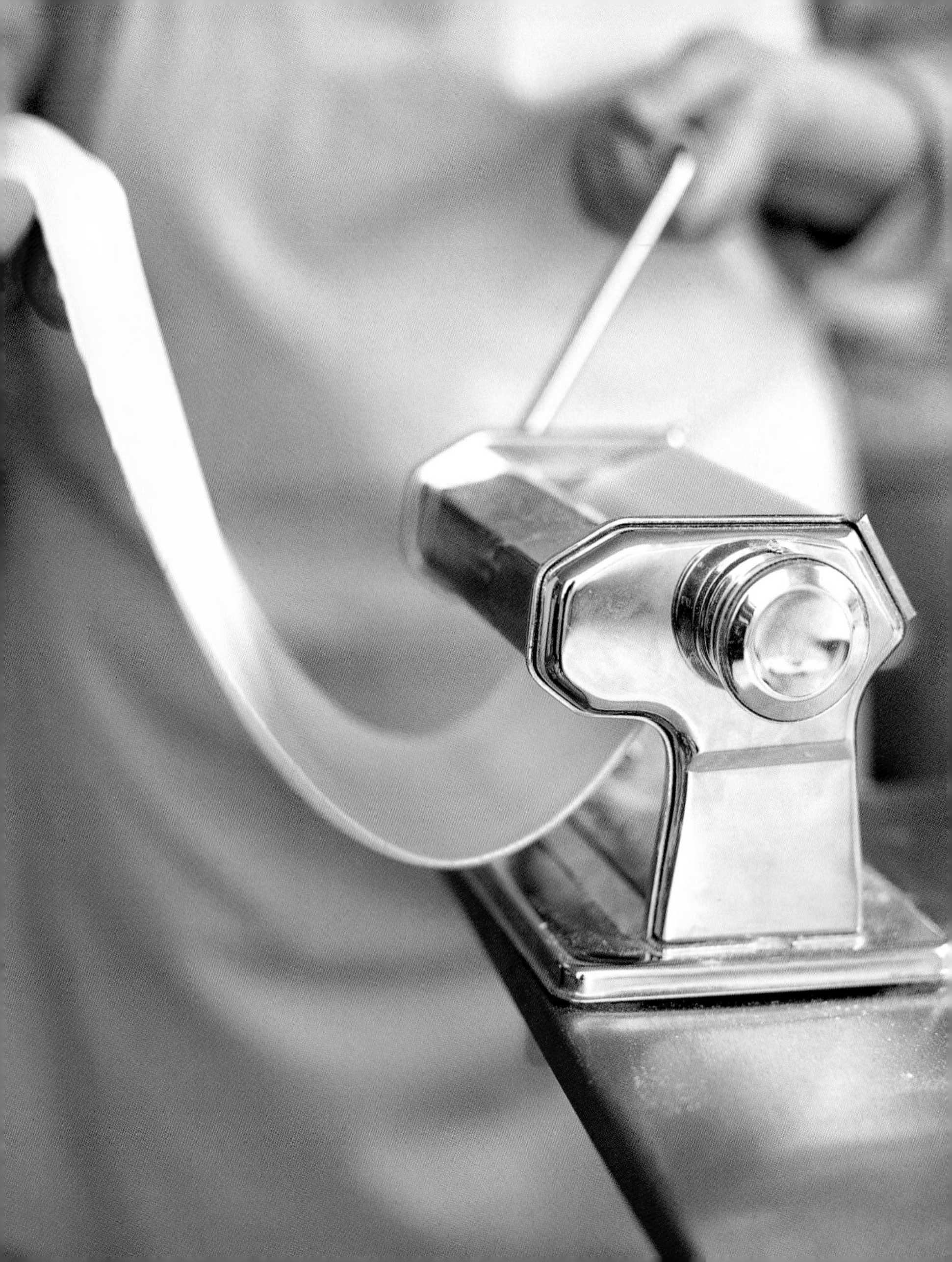

BASIC SAUCES and CLASSICS

tomato sauce with vegetables

1 kg fresh tomatoes

25 g unsalted butter

2 tablespoons olive oil

1 small celery stalk, finely chopped

1 small carrot, finely chopped

1 small onion, finely chopped

a small bunch of basil or other fresh herbs, chopped

500 g pasta, such as fusilli, or stuffed pasta, freshly cooked

sea salt and freshly ground black pepper

TO SERVE

freshly grated Parmesan cheese

a handful of fresh herbs, torn or finely chopped

extra virgin olive oil

serves 4–6

This useful base sauce begins with chopped carrot, onion and celery, which are used often in Italian cooking. It is more substantial and has a stronger flavour than the Neapolitan recipe on page 19. It is also the best recipe for non-plum tomatoes, because the vegetable base adds the extra flavour that other tomato varieties lack.

To prepare the tomatoes, cut a cross in the base of each one, and squeeze out and discard the seeds.

Heat the butter and olive oil in a heavy-based saucepan over high heat. When it starts to bubble, add the celery, carrot, onion, herbs and tomatoes. Stir quickly in the hot fat for a few minutes, then lower the heat, cover and simmer for 1 hour. Stir from time to time, adding a little water as the tomatoes reduce.

Push the sauce though a mouli (food mill) or sieve. Add salt and pepper to taste.

Toss the sauce through the freshly cooked pasta, then sprinkle with Parmesan, torn or chopped herbs and olive oil. Serve a dish of Parmesan separately for people to help themselves.

In summer, make this with fragrant ripe tomatoes – otherwise, use canned Italian plum tomatoes. The basil is added in two stages; first for depth of flavour, then at the end for a burst of fresh fragrance, hence the name double basil.

tomato sauce with double basil

- 3 tablespoons olive oil
- 2 garlic cloves, finely chopped
- 1 shallot, finely chopped
- 25 g basil leaves
- 500 g ripe tomatoes, coarsely chopped, or 400 g canned plum tomatoes
- a pinch of sugar
- 350 g pasta, such as spaghetti or linguine, freshly cooked
- sea salt and freshly ground black pepper

TO SERVE

- freshly grated Parmesan cheese
- crispy crumbs (optional)

serves 4

Heat the oil in a saucepan and add the garlic, shallot and half the basil. Cook for 3–4 minutes until the shallot is golden.

Add the tomatoes and cook, stirring, for 10 minutes, until thickened and pulpy. Add the sugar, 100 ml water and salt and pepper to taste.

Bring to the boil, cover and simmer very gently for 1 hour until dark red and thickened, with droplets of oil on the surface.

Tear the remaining basil into the tomato sauce and add the sauce to the freshly cooked pasta. Toss to mix, then serve topped with Parmesan and crispy crumbs, if wished.

Variation: crispy crumbs

These make a great addition to any tomato-based pasta sauce. Heat a couple of tablespoons of olive oil in a frying pan and add a good handful or two of fresh white breadcrumbs. Cook over a high heat, stirring, until golden brown. The smaller crumbs will char a little at the bottom of the pan, but that's good. Serve straight from the pan, sprinkled on top of the pasta, while the crumbs are still hot and sizzling.

quick neapolitan tomato sauce

1 kg canned plum tomatoes, deseeded, drained (reserve the juice) and chopped

5 tablespoons extra virgin olive oil

4 garlic cloves

your choice of:
1 small piece of fresh chilli, ½ cinnamon stick, ½ teaspoon dried oregano, or a bunch of fresh herbs such as basil

500 g pasta or stuffed pasta, freshly cooked

3 tablespoons freshly grated Parmesan cheese

sea salt and freshly ground black pepper

TO SERVE

a handful of fresh herbs, torn or finely chopped (optional)

freshly grated Parmesan cheese

extra virgin olive oil

serves 4–6

This classic tomato sauce comes originally from Campania, the region around Naples. It is made simply with canned plum tomatoes, olive oil, garlic and the flavouring of your choice, making it a handy standby – just add whatever seasoning you have to hand.

Put the prepared tomatoes, oil and garlic in a heavy-based saucepan. Add your choice of the chilli, cinnamon or herb. Cover and simmer over low heat for 30 minutes, or until the tomatoes are reduced to a creamy mass. Stir from time to time to stop the sauce sticking to the bottom of the pan. Add a little of the reserved tomato juice whenever necessary to keep the sauce moist.

Discard the garlic cloves and chilli, cinnamon or herb bunch, if used. Mash the sauce with a potato masher. If using fresh herbs, it may be necessary to purée the sauce in a blender. Taste and adjust the seasoning with salt and pepper.

Pour the sauce over the freshly cooked pasta, add the Parmesan and stir well. Transfer to a serving dish, sprinkle with fresh herbs, if using, then serve at once with extra cheese and olive oil.

Variation Chop a mozzarella cheese into small cubes and stir into the pasta at the same time as the Parmesan. Add a handful of torn basil leaves to the bowl and stir well before serving.

cream sauce with butter and parmesan

250 ml single cream

25 g unsalted butter

3 tablespoons freshly grated Parmesan cheese

lots of freshly ground black pepper or freshly grated nutmeg

50–100 ml pasta cooking water or stock

250 g egg-based pasta or stuffed pasta, freshly cooked

TO SERVE (OPTIONAL)

freshly grated Parmesan cheese

3 tablespoons finely chopped fresh herbs, such as parsley, fennel, coriander or basil

freshly grated zest of ½ unwaxed lemon

serves 4

This cream sauce enriched with cheese, herbs or citrus zest is delicious on its own, simply stirred into egg-based or stuffed pasta. It is also useful as a base – just add smoked fish or meat, cooked poultry or game, lightly boiled vegetables, herbs or nuts, to create a feast. Just about any cheese goes well with pasta.

Put the cream and butter in a shallow saucepan over low heat. Bring to simmering point, shaking the pan from time to time. Let simmer for a few minutes or until the sauce starts to thicken. Add the cheese and pepper or nutmeg and stir.

Stir the sauce and 50 ml cooking water or stock into the freshly cooked pasta. Mix until well coated. If necessary, add extra water or stock and stir again.

Serve at once with extra Parmesan, chopped herbs and grated lemon zest, if using. Dress the pasta in a bowl rather than the pan, because the heat of the pan will dry out a dairy-based sauce.

Variation Add 100 g thinly sliced smoked salmon or trout and 3 tablespoons finely chopped dill or fennel to the pasta at the same time as the cream sauce, and stir gently.

In Abruzzo, where this dish is from, the local chillies it contains are called *diavolini* – little devils. If you like spicy and simple food, this is for you, but it must be made with best-quality ingredients. Make the dressing swiftly, cook the pasta al dente, and serve straight away.

garlic, olive oil and chilli sauce

350 g pasta, such spaghettini or penne, freshly cooked

150 ml very best olive oil

4 garlic cloves

1 small to medium dried chilli (to taste), finely chopped

2 handfuls of fresh parsley, finely chopped

freshly grated Parmesan cheese, to serve (optional)

serves 4–6 as a starter

While the pasta is boiling, slowly heat the olive oil in a frying pan with the garlic and chilli. When the garlic cloves turn golden, discard them. Drain the pasta, then return it to the pan. Add the hot flavoured oil, chilli pieces and chopped parsley and stir well. Serve at once, with Parmesan, if using.

Variation For spice lovers, Arrabbiata Sauce is a tomato-based version of this recipe. (The word arrabbiata means 'angry'.) Use the Quick Neapolitan Tomato Sauce recipe on page 19, but double the amount of garlic and chillies. Add 2 handfuls of parsley, finely chopped, at the end.

bolognese

10 g dried porcini mushrooms, rinsed
1 tablespoon olive oil
1 onion, finely chopped
500 g beef mince
50 g Parma ham, coarsely chopped
100 ml Marsala or sherry
700 ml tomato passata
300 g pasta, such as spaghetti or linguine, freshly cooked
sea salt and freshly ground black pepper
fresh shavings of Parmesan cheese, to serve

serves 4

Like many classic recipes, there are countless versions of Bolognese Sauce. Some Italian chefs add sweetbreads, chicken livers and veal, but this version contains a mixture of beef mince and Parma ham. It really benefits from being chilled overnight, so it's ideal for making the day before and gently reheating.

Put the porcini in a bowl, cover with boiling water and set aside for 20 minutes until softened.

Heat the oil in a large saucepan, add the onion and cook for 2 minutes. Add the beef mince and Parma ham and cook for 3–4 minutes, stirring, until evenly browned.

Drain the porcini and discard the soaking water. Chop the porcini, then add to the pan with the Marsala and passata. Cover and simmer for 1 hour, stirring occasionally, until rich and dark. Add salt and pepper to taste.

Divide the pasta between 4 serving plates or bowls. Top with Bolognese Sauce and Parmesan shavings, then serve.

Fresh pesto is very special and with the help of a blender, simple to make (purists use a mortar and pestle, as contact with metal can discolour the basil leaves). Make it in the spring and summer when basil is in season and sold in big leafy bunches, heavy with peppery scent. Adding a little butter helps preserve its vivid green colour.

pesto genovese

a handful of pine nuts
1 walnut half
1 small garlic clove
a pinch of salt
1 teaspoon unsalted butter
a large bunch of basil
150–200 ml olive oil
1½ tablespoons freshly grated pecorino cheese
1½ tablespoons freshly grated Parmesan cheese
500 g egg pasta, such as penne or trenette, freshly cooked, plus a little reserved cooking water

TO SERVE

extra virgin olive oil
freshly grated Parmesan cheese

serves 4–6

Put the pine nuts in a dry frying pan and heat gently until golden brown all over. Take care, because they burn easily. Remove to a plate and let cool.

When cool, put the pine nuts, walnut, garlic, salt and butter in a blender and blend well. Add the basil and blend until smooth. Add the oil and reduce to a paste, then add the two cheeses quickly at the end.

Transfer the pesto to a serving dish. Rinse out the blender with a couple of tablespoons of pasta cooking water and add to the pesto. Transfer the freshly cooked pasta to the dish of pesto, pour the olive oil over, sprinkle with Parmesan and mix well.

Variations

• Make a double quantity, store in a screw-top jar, seal with a layer of olive oil and refrigerate.

• Mix in freshly cooked spring vegetables such as asparagus spears cut into short lengths, broad beans, peas or green beans.

puttanesca

2 tablespoons olive oil
1 onion, finely chopped
2 garlic cloves, finely chopped
4 anchovy fillets in oil, drained and coarsely chopped
2 red chillies, finely chopped
4 ripe tomatoes, coarsely chopped
1 tablespoon salted capers, rinsed well and coarsely chopped
100 ml red wine
75 g small black olives
2 tablespoons chopped fresh flat leaf parsley
350 g pasta, such as gemelli or penne, freshly cooked
freshly ground black pepper
freshly grated Parmesan cheese, to serve

serves 4

Puttanesca was famously named in honour of the ladies of the night, although no one seems quite sure why. I like to think it's because the sauce has a wild and fiery character. This robust dish is perfectly matched by a full-bodied red wine.

Heat the oil in a saucepan, then add the onion, garlic, anchovies and chillies. Cook over medium heat for 4–5 minutes until softened and golden. Add the tomatoes. Cook for 3–4 minutes, stirring occasionally, until softened.

Add the capers, wine and black pepper to taste, then cover and simmer for 20 minutes.

Add the tomato sauce, olives and parsley to the pasta in its warm pan and toss to mix. Divide between 4 bowls and serve topped with grated Parmesan.

This popular sauce offers crisp, garlic-scented bacon with a stream of creamy fresh eggs setting in the warm pasta, fragrant with the scent of freshly grated Parmesan. This is one of the speciality dishes found in every simple eatery in Rome.

carbonara

- 2 whole eggs
- 5 egg yolks
- 25 g unsalted butter
- 125 ml single cream
- 6 tablespoons freshly grated Parmesan cheese, plus extra to serve
- 200 g pancetta or streaky bacon
- olive oil, for frying
- 1 garlic clove, crushed
- 500 g pasta, such as penne or spaghetti, freshly cooked
- freshly ground black pepper

serves 4–6

Put the eggs and egg yolks in a bowl and mix lightly with a fork. Add the butter, cream, grated Parmesan and lots of black pepper. Let stand without mixing.

Chop the pancetta into slivers. Cover the base of a medium frying pan with olive oil and heat through. When it starts to haze, add the pancetta. When the fat starts to run, add the crushed garlic and stir well. Continue frying until the pancetta becomes crisp and golden.

Add the pancetta and pan juices to the freshly cooked pasta and mix vigorously. Beat the egg mixture lightly with a fork and pour over the pasta. Mix well and serve at once with extra cheese and plenty of freshly ground black pepper – the butter will melt and the eggs will cook in the heat of the pasta.

The clams are the stars of this dish, but it's crucial that the sauce is smooth, which is why it is made with passata rather than canned tomatoes. Delicious as this is, it's not an elegant meal to eat, so be prepared: tie your napkin firmly round your neck and use your fingers to pick the clams from their shells.

vongole

2 tablespoons olive oil
2 garlic cloves, finely chopped
a sprig of fresh rosemary
500 ml tomato passata
½ teaspoon sugar
1 kg fresh baby clams or cockles in shells
2 tablespoons chopped fresh flat leaf parsley
300 g pasta, such as spaghetti or linguine, freshly cooked
sea salt and freshly ground black pepper

serves 4

Heat the oil in a saucepan, add the garlic and rosemary and cook for 2 minutes. Add the passata and sugar, with salt and pepper to taste. Bring to the boil, cover and simmer for 30 minutes, then remove and discard the sprig of rosemary.

Put the clams and 2 tablespoons water into another large saucepan. Cover and cook over medium heat for 4–5 minutes, shaking the pan occasionally, until all the shells have opened. Discard any that remain closed.

Strain the clam cooking juices into the tomato pan through a sieve, to remove grit. When the clams are cool enough to handle, shell half of them and discard the empty shells. Add the shelled and unshelled clams to the tomato sauce and simmer for 3–4 minutes.

Add the clam sauce and parsley to the pasta in its warm pan and toss to mix. Divide between 4 bowls and serve.

It's easy to buy lasagne that requires no precooking, but it tends to draw moisture from the sauce as it cooks, and the finished dish can be dry. It's worth the little extra effort of boiling the lasagne first.

lasagne

500 g dried lasagne sheets

1 quantity Bolognese Sauce (page 24)

300 g mozzarella cheese, diced

4 tablespoons freshly grated Parmesan cheese

sea salt and freshly ground black pepper

WHITE SAUCE

1 litre milk

1 small garlic clove

50 g butter

50 g plain flour

a baking dish, about 30 x 20 x 7 cm

serves 8

Preheat the oven to 190°C (375°F) Gas 5.

Bring a large saucepan of water to the boil. Add a pinch of salt, then the lasagne sheets, one at a time so they don't stick together. Cook for 5 minutes, then drain and tip the lasagne into a bowl of cold water. Drain again and pat dry with kitchen paper.

To make the White Sauce, put the milk and garlic in a small saucepan and heat gently until warm. Melt the butter in another saucepan, then stir in the flour and cook for 1 minute. Gradually add the warm milk, stirring constantly, to make a smooth sauce. Bring to the boil, then simmer for 2–3 minutes. Remove and discard the garlic clove. Add salt and pepper to taste.

Put 3–4 tablespoons of the Bolognese Sauce in the baking dish, spread evenly across the base of the dish and cover with a layer of lasagne. Spoon over some White Sauce and a few pieces of mozzarella and continue adding layers, starting with another layer of Bolognese Sauce and finishing with the White Sauce and mozzarella, until all the ingredients have been used. Sprinkle with freshly ground black pepper and Parmesan, then bake in the preheated oven for 30 minutes until the top is crusty and golden.

VEGETABLES

Vegetables need little cooking or adornment if they are young, sweet and fresh. There is nothing like those grown in your garden and just picked, of course. Another good option is to buy from a farm shop or farmer's market. The harvest periods are short, so relish each vegetable in its season and reinvent this recipe as the crops change.

pasta primavera

500 g green vegetables, such as green beans, asparagus, peas, broad beans or a mixture (shelled weight)

olive oil, for cooking

1 onion, finely chopped

2 tablespoons white wine

400 g ripe tomatoes, skinned, deseeded and chopped

a handful of fresh mint, finely chopped

a handful of fresh basil, finely chopped

400 g pasta (any kind), freshly cooked

3 tablespoons freshly grated Parmesan cheese

80 g Parma ham, cut into strips (optional)

sea salt and freshly ground black pepper

basil leaves, to serve

serves 4

If using asparagus or green beans, cut them into 2–3 cm lengths. Cover the base of a frying pan with olive oil and heat gently. Add the onion and fry gently until softened and translucent. Add the wine and let bubble until evaporated. Stir in the green vegetables and tomatoes, then add salt and pepper to taste. Stir again, cover with a lid and cook for 10–20 minutes or until tender. Stir in the herbs, then taste again for seasoning.

Add the sauce to the freshly cooked pasta, then add the grated Parmesan and strips of Parma ham, if using. Stir well and serve topped with basil leaves.

Variations

• Vary the vegetables and herbs according to season. Try young carrots with spring cabbage, 1 teaspoon crushed juniper berries and 1 teaspoon chopped fresh thyme.

• Omit the Parma ham and use 50 g sun-dried tomatoes, thinly sliced, 1½ tablespoons capers and 1½ tablespoons olives.

• Omit the Parma ham and add 1 tablespoon finely chopped anchovies, the finely grated zest of 1 small unwaxed lemon and a handful of fresh parsley, finely chopped.

roasted vegetable sauce with capers and cherry tomatoes

1 small aubergine, about 100 g
1 red pepper, halved and deseeded
1 yellow pepper, halved and deseeded
100 g courgettes
100 g leeks, split and well washed
1½ tablespoons finely chopped fresh rosemary
2 garlic cloves, finely chopped
2 tablespoons olive oil
1–2 tablespoons capers, rinsed and drained
100 g cherry tomatoes
400 g pasta, such as ridged penne or tubetti, freshly cooked

TO SERVE

extra virgin olive oil
6 sprigs of rosemary
freshly grated Parmesan cheese

serves 4

When choosing peppers, aubergines and courgettes, squeeze them lightly to ensure the flesh is firm. When buying leeks, look for a good proportion of white trunk, the really tender, sweet part. The leaves needn't be wasted, however – providing they are fresh, just cut them off and use them to make stock.

Preheat the oven to 200°C (400°F) Gas 6.

Cut the aubergine, peppers, courgettes and leeks into bite-sized pieces, about 2 cm square, and arrange in a single layer in a roasting tin. Add the rosemary, garlic and olive oil and mix well with your hands. Cover with foil, transfer to the preheated oven and roast for 20–30 minutes until tender.

Remove and discard the foil, add the capers and cherry tomatoes, stir well and roast for a further 10 minutes.

Add the roasted vegetables to the freshly cooked pasta, stir well and spread out on a serving plate. Sprinkle with oil and rosemary and serve with Parmesan.

Variations

- Instead of cherry tomatoes, add 3 tablespoons black olives.
- Experiment with other kinds of vegetables.

courgette and toasted pine nut dressing

a handful of pine nuts, about 25 g

100 ml good olive oil

1 garlic clove

400 g baby courgettes, thinly sliced

400 g spaghettini, freshly cooked

sea salt and freshly ground black pepper

a handful of fresh parsley, finely chopped, to serve

serves 4

This recipe comes originally from Sicily, where the colourful regional cooking abounds with vegetable-based recipes enhanced by the island's glorious olive oil. The quality of the oil in this dish is as important as the freshness of the courgettes, so use something special when you make this.

Put the pine nuts in a dry frying pan and heat gently until golden brown all over. Take care, because they burn easily. Remove to a plate and let cool.

Heat the olive oil and garlic in a large frying pan and, when the garlic starts to turn golden, discard it. Add the courgettes and stir-fry quickly until golden. Add salt and pepper to taste.

Add the courgettes and their cooking oil to the freshly cooked pasta. Stir well, sprinkle with chopped parsley and the toasted pine nuts and serve.

chilli and black bean sauce with garlic-fried breadcrumbs

150 g small dried black turtle beans or 400 g canned black beans

olive oil, for cooking

1 carrot, finely chopped

1 small onion, finely chopped

½ celery stalk, finely chopped

2 garlic cloves, crushed

400 g canned plum tomatoes, drained (reserve the juice), deseeded and chopped

a small piece of dried chilli or ½ cinnamon stick

50 g rocket

250 g pasta, such as small tubetti, spirali or penne, freshly cooked

sea salt and freshly ground black pepper

50 g Parmesan cheese shavings, to serve

GARLIC-FRIED BREADCRUMBS

3 tablespoons olive oil

25 g fresh breadcrumbs

1 teaspoon finely chopped fresh rosemary

1 garlic clove, finely chopped

serves 4–6 as a starter

Turtle beans are small, black and perfectly formed, the culinary equivalent of the little black dress. With tomato sauce and garlicky breadcrumbs, they make a nutritious and satisfying pasta topping.

If using dried beans, soak them overnight in plenty of cold water. Next day, drain them, rinse well, put in a saucepan, cover with cold water and bring to the boil. Do not add salt. Boil hard for 15 minutes, then drain and rinse. If using canned beans, drain and rinse them.

Cover the base of a saucepan with olive oil, then heat gently. Add the carrot, onion, celery, garlic and beans and stir gently in the oil for 5 minutes, or until the vegetables soften. Add the tomatoes and chilli or cinnamon and stir again. Heat to simmering, cover with a lid and cook over very low heat for 30 minutes, stirring from time to time. It may be necessary to add a little reserved tomato juice to keep the sauce moist. Add salt and pepper to taste and discard the chilli or cinnamon stick.

To make the garlic-fried breadcrumbs, heat the 3 tablespoons olive oil in a frying pan. Put the breadcrumbs, rosemary and garlic in a bowl and mix well. When the oil starts to haze, add the breadcrumb mixture and fry until crisp and golden. Transfer to a plate lined with kitchen paper, let drain and cool.

Add the sauce and rocket to the freshly cooked pasta and stir well. Serve topped with garlic-fried breadcrumbs and Parmesan shavings.

calabrese and broccoli arabesque

50 g pine nuts, plus extra to serve

50 g sultanas

750 g brassica vegetables, such as calabrese, purple sprouting broccoli, or cauliflower, separated into florets, or a mixture

1½ tablespoons tomato purée

100 ml warm water

100 ml olive oil

1 onion, finely sliced

1 small can anchovies, about 50 g, drained thoroughly and patted dry with kitchen paper

50 ml scalding hot milk

400 g pasta, such as orecchiette or spaghettini, freshly cooked

torn fresh coriander leaves or fresh parsley

freshly grated pecorino or Parmesan cheese, to serve

serves 4

This unusual vegetable sauce, enhanced with sultanas, anchovies and pine nuts, explodes with flavours. It can also be served as a side dish with meat and fish. There is a huge selection of brassicas to choose from, so try one or more types and vary them according to season.

Put the pine nuts in a dry frying pan and heat gently until golden brown all over. Take care, because they burn easily. Remove to a plate and let cool.

Soak the sultanas in boiling water for 15 minutes, then drain and pat dry with kitchen paper. Cook the vegetables in a large pan of boiling salted water until just soft, 5–10 minutes. Drain well.

Put the tomato purée in a small bowl, add the warm water and stir to dilute. Heat half the olive oil in a sauté pan, then add the onion and the tomato purée mixture. Cook over low heat until softened, then add the boiled vegetables.

Mash the anchovies in a small bowl, then stir in the hot milk and remaining olive oil to form a smooth paste. Pour this over the vegetables, add the sultanas and pine nuts, stir well and cover with a lid. Turn off the heat and set aside to develop the flavours.

When you are ready to eat, add the sauce (warmed if necessary) to the freshly cooked pasta, stir well, then transfer to a large serving dish. Add the coriander and extra pine nuts. Serve at once with grated pecorino.

mushroom cream sauce with marsala

50 g unsalted butter

1 garlic clove, crushed

a handful of fresh parsley, chopped

250 g closed mushrooms, thinly sliced

40 ml Marsala or sherry

125 ml vegetable or chicken stock

250 ml single cream

3 tablespoons freshly grated Parmesan cheese, plus extra, to serve

250 g pasta, such as pappardelle, tagliatelle, fettucine or farfalle, freshly cooked

sea salt and freshly ground black pepper

chopped fresh parsley, to sprinkle

serves 4

This rich, aromatic cream sauce is flavoured with mushrooms, ever-so-slowly cooked in garlic, parsley and Marsala. The sauce also goes well with pan-fried steak, veal and pork. Keep a bottle of Marsala in the cupboard for cooking – it has a very distinctive flavour and is useful for both sweet and savoury dishes.

Melt the butter in a frying pan. Add the garlic, parsley and mushrooms and cook gently over low heat, stirring from time to time. When the mushrooms have reduced and are starting to soften, add the Marsala and salt and pepper to taste. Stir well, cover the pan with a lid and let cook for a further 30 minutes, adding a little stock from time to time. The mushrooms should be moist, but not watery. Add the cream and heat gently, shaking the pan occasionally.

Add the sauce and 3 tablespoons Parmesan to the freshly cooked pasta. Sprinkle with chopped parsley and serve at once with extra Parmesan.

Variation Cook small cubes of aubergine instead of mushrooms.

cherry tomato and mozzarella pasta with rocket

200 g baby mozzarella cheeses, halved

250 g cherry tomatoes, halved

4 tablespoons good olive oil

500 g pasta, such as small fat tubetti or farfalle, freshly cooked

50 g rocket

extra virgin olive oil, to sprinkle

balsamic vinegar, to sprinkle

sea salt and freshly ground black pepper

serves 4–6

This colourful summer dish is perfect for alfresco eating. It is more a salad than a sauce – just stir it into hot pasta and serve warm.

Put the mozzarella and cherry tomatoes in a large bowl. Add the olive oil, plenty of salt and freshly ground black pepper to taste, then mix.

Add the hot pasta to the mozzarella salad and mix well. Add the rocket, turn once, then spoon onto a flat serving dish. Sprinkle with olive oil and balsamic vinegar and serve warm.

Variation Add toasted pine nuts or finely chopped garlic to the mozzarella and tomatoes. Chop 2 handfuls parsley, mint and basil, and use instead of the rocket. Omit the balsamic vinegar.

ricotta, cinnamon and walnut sauce

250 g ricotta cheese

75 g unsalted butter, softened

1 teaspoon icing sugar

1 teaspoon ground cinnamon or mixed spice

100 ml pasta cooking water

500 g pasta, such as spaghettini, linguine or rigatoni, freshly cooked

5 tablespoons chopped walnuts

sea salt and freshly ground black pepper

TO SERVE

1½ tablespoons chopped walnuts

freshly grated Parmesan cheese

serves 4–6

A delicate and original starter for a party and an ideal vegetarian meal, this is more a dressing than a sauce, because there is no cooking. It can be prepared in the time it takes to cook the pasta. The combination of savoury and sweet elements such as cheese and sweet spices dates back to Roman times.

Put the ricotta, butter, icing sugar and cinnamon in a bowl and beat with a wooden spoon until smooth and creamy. Add salt and pepper to taste and stir in half the pasta water.

Add the ricotta mixture to the pasta, add the remaining pasta water if necessary, then stir in the chopped walnuts. Mix well until coated. Serve at once, topped with extra walnuts and Parmesan.

Variation Try toasted pine nuts or almonds instead of walnuts.

creamy vodka sauce

1 tablespoon butter

2 plum tomatoes, coarsely chopped

1 garlic clove, finely chopped

4 tablespoons chilli vodka

150 ml double cream

250 g pasta, such as fusilli or fusilli bucati, freshly cooked

sea salt and freshly ground black pepper

TO SERVE

a few fresh chives, halved

freshly grated Parmesan cheese

serves 2

Vodka and tomato is a classic combination - think of the Bloody Mary - and here they make a creamy, mild sauce (left in the picture) that you can make in the time it takes to boil the pasta. If you haven't got chilli vodka, add a small, finely chopped chilli at the same time as the garlic and use ordinary vodka.

Heat the butter in a small saucepan, add the tomatoes and garlic and cook for 3 minutes. Add the vodka and boil rapidly for 2 minutes. Reduce the heat and simmer for 2–3 minutes, then stir in the cream and simmer gently for a further 5 minutes. Add salt and pepper to taste.

Add the creamy sauce to the pasta in its warm pan and mix well. Transfer to 2 serving bowls and top with chives. Sprinkle with plenty of Parmesan and black pepper and serve.

All you need to make this delicious variation on the classic basil pesto is fresh broccoli and a few storecupboard ingredients. The chilli and lemon give it a refreshing bite.

broccoli and pine nut pesto

175 g broccoli florets
2 tablespoons pine nuts
3 tablespoons olive oil
3 garlic cloves, finely chopped
1 red chilli, deseeded and finely chopped
½ lemon
175 g pasta, such as penne or fusilli, freshly cooked
sea salt and freshly ground black pepper
fresh shavings of Parmesan cheese, to serve

serves 2

Cook the broccoli in boiling, salted water for 10–12 minutes until very soft. Meanwhile, heat a dry frying pan until hot, add the pine nuts and cook, turning them frequently, until golden and toasted. Transfer to a plate and set aside.

Heat the olive oil in a small saucepan and add the garlic and chilli. Gently cook for 2–3 minutes until softened. Remove from the heat and set aside.

Drain the broccoli, return it to the pan and mash coarsely with a fork. Add the garlic and chilli oil and toasted pine nuts. Mix well, squeeze in a little juice from the half lemon and add salt and pepper to taste. Combine with the freshly cooked pasta.

Divide between 2 serving bowls, top with fresh Parmesan shavings and extra black pepper, and serve.

Roasted aubergine adds a deliciously sweet, silky texture to sauces, and it is superb at absorbing the flavour and texture of olive oil. The rich taste of the roasted vegetables and the tangy herbs belie the simplicity of this easy-to-make dish.

roasted aubergine and tomato sauce

2 aubergines, cut into 3 cm cubes

500 g ripe tomatoes, quartered

2 garlic cloves, halved

4 tablespoons olive oil

300 g pasta, such as fusilli or fusilli bucati, freshly cooked

1 shallot, finely chopped

2 tablespoons chopped fresh mint

2 tablespoons chopped fresh coriander

freshly squeezed juice of 1 lime

sea salt and freshly ground black pepper

serves 4

Preheat the oven to 200°C (400°F) Gas 6.

Put the aubergines, tomatoes and garlic in a large roasting tin. Add 2 tablespoons of the olive oil and mix. Sprinkle with salt and pepper and cook in the preheated oven for 30–40 minutes, turning the vegetables from time to time, until the aubergine is tender and golden.

Add the roasted aubergine and tomatoes to the freshly cooked pasta, then the shallot, mint, coriander and lime juice. Add the remaining oil and toss well to mix. Divide between 4 bowls or plates and serve.

salsa verde with char-grilled cheese

1 tablespoon olive oil
2 tablespoons plain flour
1 teaspoon cracked black pepper
250 g halloumi or provolone cheese, cut into 1 cm slices
300 g pasta, such as fusilli, freshly cooked

SALSA VERDE
2 anchovy fillets in oil, drained
1 tablespoon salted capers, rinsed well
1 green chilli, deseeded and finely chopped
1 garlic clove, crushed
3 tablespoons chopped fresh flat leaf parsley
1 tablespoon chopped fresh coriander
2 teaspoons Dijon mustard
3 tablespoons olive oil
1 tablespoon white wine vinegar

a stove-top grill pan

serves 4

You can vary the salsa verde according to the herbs you have to hand. Parsley should always be the base, but feel free to add basil, tarragon or mint instead of the coriander. The salsa verde makes a fine pasta sauce without the cheese, if you want a lighter meal.

To make the Salsa Verde, chop the anchovy fillets and capers finely using a heavy knife. Put the chilli and garlic on top and chop again until very finely chopped. Transfer to a bowl and add the herbs, mustard, oil and vinegar.

To cook the cheese, heat 1 tablespoon oil in a stove-top grill pan until hot. Put the flour on a small plate, add the black pepper and mix. Dip each cheese slice in the flour to coat on both sides, shaking off any excess. Cook in the grill pan for 1–2 minutes on each side until golden brown, then drain on kitchen paper.

Add the Salsa Verde to the freshly cooked pasta and toss to mix. Divide between 4 bowls or plates, arrange the cheese on top, then serve.

sage, lemon and mozzarella butter with roasted pumpkin

Tantalizing pockets of melting garlic butter flavoured with herbs and cheese complement the succulent roast pumpkin in this dish. The flavoured butter also makes brilliant garlic bread – it melts to become a deliciously moist and stretchy topping.

2 tablespoons olive oil

500 g pumpkin or butternut squash

1 teaspoon cumin seeds

150 g mozzarella cheese, coarsely chopped

50 g butter, softened

2 garlic cloves, crushed

2 teaspoons chopped fresh sage leaves, plus extra whole leaves, to serve

grated zest and freshly squeezed juice of 1 unwaxed lemon

300 g pasta, such as fusilli bucati or cavatappi, freshly cooked

sea salt and freshly ground black pepper

serves 4

Preheat the oven to 200°C (400°F) Gas 6.

Put the olive oil in a roasting tin and transfer to the preheated oven for 5 minutes, until hot.

Using a small, sharp knife, peel the pumpkin, remove the seeds and cut the flesh into cubes, about 2.5 cm.

Add the cumin seeds to the hot oil in the roasting tin, then add the pumpkin and salt and pepper to taste. Toss to coat. Roast in the oven for 30 minutes, turning from time to time until tender and golden brown.

Put the mozzarella, butter, garlic, sage, lemon zest and juice, and salt and pepper in a food processor. Blend to a coarse paste. Transfer to a sheet of greaseproof paper and roll into a cylinder. Chill for at least 20 minutes or until firm enough to slice.

Add the roasted pumpkin to the freshly cooked pasta. Slice or dice the mozzarella butter and add to the pumpkin and pasta. Toss, divide between 4 bowls or plates, top with sage leaves and serve.

This is a simplified version of that old favourite, macaroni cheese, but incredibly easy to make. With no flour, there's no risk of lumps in the sauce, either.

three cheese baked penne

350 g penne, freshly cooked

400 g mascarpone cheese

2 tablespoons wholegrain mustard

300 g Fontina cheese, grated

4 tablespoons freshly grated Parmesan cheese

sea salt and freshly ground black pepper

a baking dish, about 30 x 20 cm

serves 4

Preheat the oven to 200°C (400°F) Gas 6.

Mix the freshly cooked pasta and mascarpone. Add the mustard, Fontina and Parmesan, and salt and pepper to taste. Stir to mix.

Transfer to the baking dish and cook in the preheated oven for 25–30 minutes until golden and bubbling.

FISH and SEAFOOD

fishmarket sauce

300 g small clams, in the shell

300 g mussels, in the shell

300 g small squid

300 g prawns

other fish or seafood, to taste

olive oil, for cooking

a handful of fresh parsley, chopped

a piece of dried chilli, to taste

4 garlic cloves, finely chopped

150 ml white wine

500 g spaghettini, freshly cooked

sea salt and freshly ground black pepper

TO SERVE

a handful of fresh parsley, finely chopped

extra virgin olive oil

serves 4–6

This is the mother of all seafood sauces, a favourite in practically every beach and harbour restaurant in Italy. Its success depends very much on the freshness and variety of the fish, so try it anywhere there's a good fish market. You can also stir this sauce into risotto, or serve it with bread.

Clean the fish and seafood as necessary. Scrub the clams and mussels, rinse thoroughly in cold running water and drain well. Discard any that remain open. Cut the squid into rings (very small squid can be cooked whole).

Cover the base of a large frying pan or large saucepan with olive oil, then set over medium heat. Add the chopped parsley, chilli and garlic and cook until soft. Increase the heat, add the white wine and let bubble until evaporated.

Add the squid and fry for a few minutes, then add the clams and mussels, cover and shake the pan until all the shells have opened (discard any that will not open). Add the prawns and cook for a few more minutes until they become opaque – no longer, or they will be tough and tasteless. Add salt and pepper to taste. Remove the pan from the heat and set aside, with the lid on, to develop the flavours.

Add half the sauce to the freshly cooked pasta and mix well. Spoon the remaining sauce on top, add the chopped parsley and olive oil and serve at once.

monkfish and italian vegetable sauce

500 g monkfish tail

4 tablespoons good olive oil, plus extra for roasting

2 shallots, finely chopped

300 g baby courgettes, cut into bite-sized pieces

300 g red peppers, halved, deseeded and cut into bite-sized pieces

125 ml white wine

2½ tablespoons capers

250 g tomatoes, skinned, deseeded and chopped

1½ tablespoons pitted black olives

500 g pasta, such as farfalle or tagliatelle, freshly cooked

sea salt and freshly ground black pepper

TO SERVE

25 basil leaves or a handful of fresh parsley, finely chopped

extra virgin olive oil

a shallow roasting tin, oiled

serves 4–6

Although tomato is a perennially popular base for pasta sauces, too much will mask the taste of the fish, so tomatoes are used sparingly here along with other vegetables.

Preheat the oven to 200°C (400°F) Gas 6.

Wipe the fish and cut into 4 equal pieces, discarding any bones. Season well with salt and pepper, arrange in the oiled roasting tin and set aside.

Heat the oil in a frying pan, then add the shallots. Cook until soft, then raise the heat, add the courgettes and peppers and brown quickly. Add the wine and, when it has evaporated, add the capers. Stir well, then add salt and pepper to taste.

Spoon the cooked vegetables over the fish in the roasting tin until covered. Add the chopped tomatoes, olives and extra olive oil. Cover the tin with foil and cook in the preheated oven for 8 minutes. Remove from the oven, discard the foil, cut the fish into bite-sized pieces and mix carefully into the vegetables.

Add the fish, vegetables and their cooking juices to the freshly cooked pasta and mix well, then stir in the basil or parsley and oil and serve.

Variations

- Try thick cod, halibut, salmon or haddock fillets rather than monkfish tails.
- Use leeks, fennel bulbs, mushrooms and aubergines instead of peppers and courgettes.

This is a delicious lunch or supper dish made with ingredients that, although not all strictly from the storecupboard, are to be found in most kitchens.

tuna, coriander and lemon dressing with tomato salad

olive oil, for cooking

2 onions, finely sliced

1 teaspoon crushed coriander seeds

2 cans of tuna in oil, 160 g each, lightly drained

1½ tablespoons capers (optional)

grated zest of 1 unwaxed lemon

125 ml milk

500 g pasta, such as tagliatelle, freshly cooked

a handful of fresh mint sprigs, to serve

TOMATO SALAD

4 firm tomatoes, skinned, deseeded and chopped small

3 tablespoons olive oil

1½ tablespoons chopped fresh mint or parsley

sea salt and freshly ground black pepper

serves 4–6

To prepare the salad, mix the tomatoes with the oil, mint and salt and pepper to taste and set aside to develop the flavours.

To make the sauce, cover the base of a frying pan with olive oil, add the onions and coriander seeds and cook slowly over medium heat. When the onions start to soften, add 3 tablespoons water and cover with a lid. Continue cooking over low heat until soft. This will take 15 minutes – do not rush, and add extra water if necessary.

When the onions are very soft, add the tuna, capers, if using, lemon zest, lots of black pepper and half the milk. Stir well, cover again and cook for 10 minutes over low heat, adding the remaining milk if necessary.

Add the sauce and tomato salad to the freshly cooked pasta and mix well. Serve at once, sprinkled with mint sprigs.

Variation Use 300 g cherry tomatoes, cut in half, instead of the tomato salad.

Spaghettini with clams is typical of almost every coastal region of Italy. It comes in two versions; *in bianco* (in oil, garlic and parsley), as here, or *al pomodoro* (with tomato sauce). You can also make an easy storecupboard version of this, using jars of clams and canned Italian tomatoes.

baby clam sauce

1 kg small fresh clams, in their shells

125–150 ml olive oil

1 garlic clove

a piece of dried chilli

2 handfuls of fresh parsley, finely chopped

500 g spaghettini, freshly cooked

TO SERVE

freshly ground black pepper

finely chopped fresh parsley

extra virgin olive oil

serves 4–6

Wash the clams in plenty of running water until not a trace of sand is left. Drain well. Put them in a heavy-based saucepan over high heat. Cover with a lid and shake the pan until all the clams have opened. Strain off the liquid released by the clams, pour it through a fine sieve and reserve. Reduce the juices if you think they are going to drown the clams excessively.

Heat the olive oil in a large saucepan, add the garlic and chilli and heat gently. When the garlic clove starts to turn golden, discard it and the chilli. Add the clams to the pan, together with their strained cooking liquid. Add the parsley and cook gently for a minute or two for the flavours to blend.

Add the clams to the freshly cooked spaghettini and mix well. Tip onto a large serving plate and top with lots of black pepper, some more parsley and olive oil. Serve at once.

Variation To make the clam sauce with tomatoes, skin, deseed and chop 500 g plum tomatoes, then add to the oil at the same time as the garlic and chilli. Cook over low heat for 20–30 minutes until reduced to a creamy mass. Add the clams and the strained juices and cook for a minute or so for the flavours to blend. Discard the garlic and chilli if preferred. Add the parsley and proceed as in the main recipe.

grilled prawns and salmon with basil citrus sauce

100 g cooked prawns, shelled

200 ml single cream

50 g unsalted butter

200 g thick salmon fillet, cut into thin slices across the grain of the fish

olive oil, to taste

finely grated zest of 1 unwaxed lemon and freshly squeezed juice of ½

150 g small uncooked prawn tails, shell on, such as Icelandic prawns

20 basil leaves, finely sliced

300 g egg pasta, such as farfalle, pappardelle or tagliatelle, freshly cooked

sea salt and freshly ground black pepper

a stove-top grill pan

serves 4

Lemon zest and juice cut through the richness of this creamy sauce with char-grilled seafood. It is luxurious enough to be an excellent choice to serve to dinner guests.

Put the shelled prawns in a food processor and blend to a paste. Put the cream, butter and freshly ground black pepper in a small saucepan and heat gently, shaking the pan from time to time. When the sauce has thickened, add the prawn paste to the cream, stir, cover and switch off the heat.

Heat a stove-top grill pan until very hot. Arrange the strips of salmon across the ridges of the pan and cook quickly on both sides. Transfer the pieces to a plate as they brown, and sprinkle with oil, lemon juice, salt and pepper.

Pan-grill the unshelled prawns, in batches if necessary, until aromatic and opaque. Do not overcook or they will be tough and tasteless. Set aside 8 prawns and 4 slices of the salmon for serving.

Add the sauce, salmon pieces, prawns and basil to the freshly cooked pasta and mix well. Divide between 4 bowls. Put 2 reserved prawns and a slice of salmon on top of each portion and sprinkle with lemon zest. Serve at once.

seafood spaghettini

4–5 tablespoons olive oil

1 garlic clove, finely chopped

300 g mixed seafood, such as squid, cut into rings; shelled prawns; and scallops, halved crossways

500 g fresh mussels, scrubbed and debearded, or clams in shells, scrubbed

2 tablespoons chopped fresh flat leaf parsley

300 g spaghettini or spaghetti, freshly cooked

sea salt and freshly ground black pepper

serves 4

Vary the seafood depending on what's available and best on the day, but always include clams or mussels – for their flavour as well as their beautiful shells.

Heat half the oil in a large sauté pan or saucepan and cook the garlic without letting it brown. Add the mixed seafood and cook for 3–4 minutes, stirring constantly, until just cooked. Transfer to a large bowl and set aside.

Add the mussels or clams to the seafood pan, cover with a lid and cook for 5 minutes until all the shells have opened. Discard any that remain closed.

Add the mussels or clams, seafood, remaining olive oil and parsley to the freshly cooked pasta. Add salt and pepper to taste, toss gently to mix, then serve.

A delicious, low-fat pasta dish. Better still, it's ready to serve in the time it takes to cook the linguine.

mussels in white wine with linguine

150 ml dry white wine

2 garlic cloves, finely chopped

1 red chilli, deseeded and finely chopped

1 kg fresh mussels in shells, debearded and scrubbed

2 tablespoons chopped fresh flat leaf parsley

300 g linguine or tagliatelle, freshly cooked

sea salt and freshly ground black pepper

olive oil, to serve

serves 4

Put the wine, garlic and chilli in a large saucepan, bring to the boil and simmer rapidly for 5 minutes. Add the mussels, cover with a lid and cook for 5 minutes, shaking the pan from time to time until all the shells have opened. Discard any that remain closed.

Add the parsley and the mussels to the freshly cooked pasta and toss gently to mix. Add salt and pepper to taste. Divide between 4 bowls, sprinkle with olive oil, then serve.

herbed tagliatelle with prawn skewers

20 uncooked tiger prawns, shelled but with tails on

2 garlic cloves, crushed

½ teaspoon crushed dried chillies

4 tablespoons olive oil

1 lemon, cut into wedges

1 teaspoon chopped fresh rosemary

2 tablespoons chopped fresh flat leaf parsley

1 tablespoon snipped fresh chives

a handful of rocket

350 g pasta, such as tagliatelle, linguine or fettuccine, freshly cooked

sea salt and freshly ground black pepper

4 wooden skewers, soaked in water for 30 minutes

a stove-top grill pan

serves 4

A lovely, summery dish to make the most of fragrant garden herbs. Serving the prawns on skewers adds to the sense of occasion (and makes them easier to turn while cooking), but you can always cook them loose and add to the pasta just before serving.

Put the prawns in a bowl and add the garlic, dried chillies, 1 tablespoon of the olive oil, and salt and pepper to taste. Mix well, then thread 5 prawns onto each skewer.

Preheat a stove-top grill pan until hot. Add the prawn skewers to the hot pan and cook for 3 minutes on each side until pink and cooked through. Remove and keep them warm. Add the lemon wedges to the pan and cook quickly for 30 seconds on each side.

Add the remaining oil, rosemary, parsley, chives and rocket to the freshly cooked pasta, with salt and pepper to taste. Toss gently, then divide between 4 serving bowls. Top each with a prawn skewer and a lemon wedge for squeezing, then serve.

This is one of those storecupboard dishes that saves your life when you get home late, tired and hungry. Keep a stock of anchovies, olive oil and spaghetti in the cupboard and you can always make it at short notice.

white spaghetti

6 tablespoons olive oil

4 garlic cloves, halved

6 anchovy fillets in oil, drained

150 g spaghetti, freshly cooked

sea salt and freshly ground black pepper

serves 2

Put the olive oil and garlic in a small saucepan and heat very gently over low heat for 4–5 minutes until the garlic is pale golden but not browned. Remove and discard the garlic.

Add the anchovies and 100 ml water to the pan and simmer rapidly, whisking with a fork until the anchovies have almost dissolved into the mixture. Add plenty of black pepper and a tiny pinch of salt.

Add the anchovy mixture to the freshly cooked pasta and toss well to mix. Divide between 2 bowls or plates and serve.

creamy smoked salmon sauce

300 ml double cream

2 garlic cloves, crushed

200 g smoked salmon, cut into 1 cm strips

4 tablespoons freshly grated Parmesan cheese, plus extra to serve

300 g pasta, such as fusilli bucati or farfalle, freshly cooked

sea salt and freshly ground black pepper

2 tablespoons snipped fresh chives, to serve

serves 4

Smoked fish always goes well with cream in a pasta sauce, as do scallops and fresh salmon. Smoked salmon adds a lovely delicate flavour here. Add it right at the last moment so it doesn't overcook or break into tiny pieces.

Put the cream and garlic in a small saucepan. Add salt and pepper to taste and heat gently until warmed through.

Add the cream, smoked salmon and Parmesan to the freshly cooked pasta, toss gently, then divide between 4 bowls or plates. Sprinkle with chives and extra Parmesan and serve.

Home-made pasta dough is worth the effort to show off this luxurious crab, tarragon and lemon filling. Make these very small shapes in batches, rolling out one sheet of dough at a time, so that the pasta doesn't dry out as you are working.

crab tortellini

2 tablespoons olive oil

1 shallot, finely chopped

2 garlic cloves, finely chopped

1 red chilli, deseeded and finely chopped

1 tablespoon chopped fresh tarragon, plus extra leaves to serve

grated zest and freshly squeezed juice of 1 unwaxed lemon

250 g fresh or canned white crabmeat, drained if canned

1 quantity Fresh Pasta (page 10)

50 g unsalted butter, cubed

sea salt and freshly ground black pepper

a plain pastry cutter, 5 cm diameter

serves 4

Heat the oil in a small frying pan, add the shallot, garlic and chilli and cook for 4–5 minutes until softened and golden. Remove from the heat and stir in the tarragon, half the lemon zest, the crabmeat, salt and black pepper.

Divide the pasta dough into 6 and roll out 1 piece (see page 10). Put the sheet of rolled dough onto a lightly floured surface and, using the pastry cutter, stamp out 10–12 rounds. Put a small teaspoon of the crab mixture in the centre of each circle, brush water lightly round the edge of the circle and fold over to enclose the filling. Seal, excluding as much air as possible. Bring the two tips together and pinch firmly to seal them. Working in batches, repeat with the remaining pasta dough and filling mixture.

Bring a large saucepan of water to the boil. Add a good pinch of salt, then the tortellini, and cook for 3–4 minutes until they rise to the surface and are cooked through.

Meanwhile, put the remaining lemon zest and the juice in a small saucepan over low heat. Add the butter, 1 or 2 cubes at a time, and stir with a whisk until smooth and foaming. Carefully drain the tortellini, return them to the warm pan and add the lemon butter. Stir briefly, then divide between 4 bowls or plates. Top with a few tarragon leaves and plenty of black pepper, then serve.

Note If you are not cooking the tortellini immediately, arrange them in a single layer on a tray lined with greaseproof paper, cover with another sheet of greaseproof paper and chill for up to 2 hours.

MEAT and POULTRY

amatriciana

olive oil, for cooking

200 g pancetta or streaky bacon, cut into thin strips

a piece of dried chilli, to taste

1 onion, finely chopped

800 g canned tomatoes, drained (retain the juice), deseeded and chopped

500 g pasta, such as bucatini, spaghetti or penne, freshly cooked

3 tablespoons freshly grated pecorino or Parmesan cheese, plus extra, to serve

a handful of fresh parsley, chopped

sea salt and freshly ground black pepper

extra virgin olive oil, to serve

serves 4–6

This well-known recipe is synonymous with the robust traditional cooking of Rome. The sauce is made with fried pancetta and onions, flavoured with chilli and cooked in tomato. Traditionally it is served with bucatini, thick spaghetti-like pasta with a hole running though the middle.

Cover the base of a frying pan with olive oil, then set over medium heat until a haze starts to rise. Add the pancetta and chilli. Cook until the pancetta fat runs, then add the onion. Fry over low heat until transparent.

Add the tomatoes, cover and cook over low heat for 30 minutes. Stir often to prevent sticking, adding a little of the tomato juice to the pan if necessary. Discard the chilli and add salt and pepper to taste. At this stage the sauce can be rested and reheated when required.

When ready to serve, stir the sauce into the freshly cooked pasta, and mix in 3 tablespoons cheese and the parsley. Serve at once, sprinkled with oil and extra cheese.

herbed chicken with garlic breadcrumbs

300 g boneless, skinless chicken thighs

50 g pancetta or bacon

a handful of fresh parsley

3 tablespoons olive oil

40 ml white wine

1 small garlic clove, finely chopped

1 teaspoon chopped fresh marjoram leaves or a pinch of dried marjoram

400 g canned tomatoes, drained, deseeded and chopped

500 g pasta, such as wide pappardelle, farfalle or rigatoni, freshly cooked

sea salt and freshly ground black pepper

freshly grated Parmesan cheese, to serve (optional)

GARLIC BREADCRUMBS

4 tablespoons olive oil

25 g fresh breadcrumbs

1 teaspoon finely chopped fresh marjoram

1 garlic clove, finely chopped

serves 4–6

Garlic breadcrumbs are served with pasta all over southern Italy instead of cheese, a legacy of the days when the region was very poor and there was no dairy farming to speak of. Today they make a tasty alternative to the ubiquitous Parmesan.

Cut each chicken thigh into 6–10 bite-sized pieces. Put the pancetta and parsley together and chop finely. Heat the oil in a heavy-based saucepan, add the pancetta and parsley and fry over low heat until transparent. Add the chicken pieces and fry until brown. Add the white wine and heat until evaporated. Add the garlic, marjoram, tomatoes and salt and pepper to taste. Cover with a lid and cook gently for 30 minutes. Stir from time to time. At this stage the sauce can be rested and reheated when required.

To make the garlic breadcrumbs, heat the olive oil in a frying pan. Put the breadcrumbs, chopped marjoram and garlic in a bowl and mix well. When the oil starts to haze, add the breadcrumb mixture and fry until crisp and golden. Transfer to a plate covered with kitchen paper and let drain and cool.

Add the chicken sauce to the freshly cooked pasta and mix well. Sprinkle with garlic breadcrumbs and serve with Parmesan cheese, if using.

meatballs in tomato sauce

MEATBALLS

125 g lean minced pork

50 g freshly grated pecorino cheese

75 g bread rolls, soaked in milk and squeezed dry

a handful of fresh parsley, chopped

1 small garlic clove, chopped

1 egg

1 tablespoon red wine

plain flour, for rolling

vegetable oil, for frying

sea salt and freshly ground black pepper

TOMATO SAUCE

olive oil, for cooking

1 small onion, finely chopped

1 small carrot, finely chopped

½ celery stalk, finely chopped

1 kg canned Italian plum tomatoes, drained (retain the juices), deseeded and chopped

20 fresh basil leaves, plus extra to serve

50 g freshly grated pecorino cheese, plus extra to serve

500 g pasta, such as rigatoni or orecchiete, freshly cooked

an electric deep-fat fryer (optional)

serves 4–6

Meatballs in tomato sauce are synonymous with early immigrants to the US from southern Italy – and no wonder, because the dish still plays an important part in the food of this region. This is great comfort food for a winter evening.

First make the meatballs. Put the meat, cheese, bread, parsley, garlic, egg, red wine, and salt and pepper in a bowl. Mix well and refrigerate for 1 hour.

To make the tomato sauce, cover the base of a frying pan with olive oil and heat gently. Add the onion, carrot and celery and cook over low heat until soft. Do not let brown. Add the tomatoes and basil, season with salt and pepper, cover with a lid and cook for 30 minutes. Stir from time to time, adding a little reserved tomato juice if necessary.

Take small teaspoons of the meatball mixture and roll into tiny balls, flouring your hands as you work. The meatballs may be deep-fried or shallow-fried in batches in vegetable oil. If using an electric deep-fat fryer, follow the manufacturer's instructions. As each meatball is well browned and done, remove with a slotted spoon and drain on kitchen paper. When all the meatballs have been fried and drained, put them into the tomato sauce and cook over gentle heat for 10 minutes. At this point, the sauce can be set aside and reheated when required.

When ready to serve, add the reheated sauce and the 50 g pecorino to the freshly cooked pasta, season and mix well. Scatter with basil leaves and serve with extra cheese.

Variation Use 125 g beef or veal or 100 g turkey and 25 g ham instead of pork.

meat sauce with tomato, mushrooms and pine nuts

10 g dried porcini mushrooms
milk (see method)
3 tablespoons olive oil
1 onion, finely chopped
100 g lean minced beef
25 g pine nuts
400 g canned tomatoes, drained (reserve the juices), deseeded and chopped
1 tablespoon finely chopped mixed fresh rosemary and thyme leaves, plus 1 teaspoon of each to serve
3 tablespoons freshly grated Parmesan cheese, plus extra to serve
500 g pasta, such as tagliatelle, spaghettini or ridged penne, freshly cooked
sea salt and freshly ground black pepper

serves 4–6

This light meat sauce is swelled with tomatoes, mushrooms and pine nuts, enough to dress 500 g of pasta. It's less rich than a typical Bolognese sauce and lower in fat.

Put the mushrooms in a bowl, add enough milk to cover, then soak for 15 minutes. Squeeze them dry and chop finely. Discard the milk.

Heat the olive oil in a large saucepan, add the onion and cook over low heat until soft. Increase the heat, add the meat and fry until browned. Add the pine nuts, mushrooms, tomatoes, herbs and salt and pepper, stir well and cover with a lid. Reduce the heat and cook slowly for 1 hour. Stir at regular intervals and, if necessary, add a little of the reserved tomato juice to keep the sauce moist.

Add the sauce and Parmesan to the freshly cooked pasta and mix well. Serve at once sprinkled with extra herbs. Serve the extra cheese separately.

Variation Use minced pork, veal or lean lamb instead of beef.

This version of a traditional recipe uses Italian sausages rather than pancetta as its base. There is a good contrast in flavour and texture between the coarse sausage, sweet peas and bright tomatoes.

country sausage, pea and tomato sauce

- olive oil, for cooking
- 8 coarse-textured Italian-type sausages
- 200 ml stock, such as chicken, beef or vegetable
- 1 small onion, finely chopped
- 1 kg fresh peas, shelled, or 250 g frozen peas
- 1 teaspoon icing sugar
- a handful of fresh parsley, chopped
- 200 g cherry tomatoes, halved
- 500 g pasta, such as ridged penne or tubetti, freshly cooked
- 3 tablespoons freshly grated Parmesan cheese, plus extra to serve

serves 4–6

Cover the base of a frying pan with olive oil, then set over medium heat. Add the sausages and cook over low heat, turning until they are brown on all sides. Remove from the heat, set the sausages aside and pour off and reserve the excess fat. When cool enough to handle, cut the sausages in half lengthways, scrape out the meat and discard the skins. Add a little stock to the sausage pan, return to the heat and deglaze. Add the sausage meat to the resulting pan juices, stir and simmer for a few minutes. The whole process will take 20–30 minutes.

Pour a little of the reserved sausage fat into a clean frying pan and heat through. Add the onion and cook over gentle heat until soft. Add the peas, icing sugar, parsley and enough stock to cover the ingredients. Cover with a lid and cook until the peas are tender. If using frozen peas, add them to the softened onions with 100 ml stock and heat through.

Stir the pea mixture into the sausage meat and let simmer for about 5 minutes. When ready to serve, increase the heat, add the tomatoes and cook quickly until the edges start to wilt. Add the sauce to the freshly cooked pasta, stir in the Parmesan and mix well. Serve with extra cheese.

Cold ham and salad never tasted as good as this simple supper dish. Finely shredded Savoy cabbage, leeks or bok choy can be used instead of iceberg lettuce. Vegetarians might like to add 125 g chopped walnuts instead of ham. Béchamel is a very versatile base sauce to which all kinds of ingredients can be added.

béchamel sauce with ham, emmental and salad leaves

50 g unsalted butter
25 g plain flour
250 ml warm milk
nutmeg (see method)
1 small onion, finely chopped
200 g iceberg lettuce, shredded
125 g cooked ham, sliced into thin strips
500 g pasta, such as ridged penne or farfalle, freshly cooked
60 g Emmental cheese shavings
sea salt and freshly ground black pepper
freshly grated Parmesan cheese, to serve

serves 4–6

To make the béchamel sauce, put 25 g butter in a saucepan and melt until it starts to bubble. Add the flour and mix well. Cook over gentle heat for 1–2 minutes, add the milk and continue cooking until the sauce thickens. Stir constantly with a wire whisk to stop lumps forming. Add salt and grated nutmeg to taste.

Gently melt the remaining butter in a large frying pan. Add the onion and fry over low heat until transparent. Add the lettuce and continue cooking for 5 minutes. Grate half a nutmeg onto the lettuce and onion as it is cooking. When the lettuce is well wilted, add the ham and béchamel sauce and stir. Add salt and pepper to taste.

Add the sauce to the freshly cooked pasta, mix until well coated and sprinkle with Emmental shavings. Serve the grated Parmesan separately.

Variation Instead of lettuce, use 500 g mushrooms sautéed in butter with thyme and garlic, add to the béchamel and serve with Parmesan shavings.

italian steak sauce

1 tablespoon chopped fresh rosemary

2 tablespoons chopped fresh flat leaf parsley, plus extra to serve

2 garlic cloves, crushed

4 semi-dried sunblush tomatoes or sun-dried tomatoes

2 teaspoons salted capers, rinsed well

8 minute steaks, 50 g each

1 tablespoon olive oil

800 g canned plum tomatoes

300 g pasta, such as conchiglie or rigatoni, freshly cooked

sea salt and freshly ground black pepper

kitchen string

serves 4

The traditional way to eat this would be to serve the sauce with the pasta and to follow with the steak, a selection of salads and some crusty bread. Here the steak is conveniently cut into slices and mixed with the pasta and sauce.

Put the rosemary, parsley, garlic, tomatoes and capers in a food processor and process until finely chopped.

Put the steaks flat on a work surface and sprinkle lightly with salt and freshly ground black pepper. Spread the herb mixture evenly over each steak and roll up tightly, tying string around the middle to secure.

Heat the olive oil until very hot in a large sauté pan, add the rolled steaks and cook for 2–3 minutes until browned all over. Add the canned tomatoes and salt and pepper to taste. Cover and simmer for 1 hour, then remove the lid and cook for a further 20 minutes until the meat is tender and the sauce is thickened and pulpy.

Transfer the steaks from the sauce to a chopping board. Remove and discard the string, then cut each steak crossways into chunky slices.

Add the sauce and steak to the freshly cooked pasta and toss to mix. Divide between 4 bowls or plates, top with chopped parsley and serve.

pancetta and chicken meatballs

500 g chicken mince

50 g thinly sliced pancetta, coarsely chopped

6 spring onions, finely chopped

4 garlic cloves, finely chopped

2 red chillies, deseeded and finely chopped

4 tablespoons freshly grated Parmesan cheese, plus extra to serve

1 tablespoon fresh thyme leaves

1 tablespoon olive oil

200 ml red wine

800 g canned plum tomatoes

a pinch of sugar

300 g pasta, such as conchiglie or gnocchi, freshly cooked

sea salt and freshly ground black pepper

serves 4

Meatballs are a time-honoured accompaniment to pasta. These delicious little mouthfuls are made with chicken, bacon and herbs, so are somewhat lighter than the traditional all-meat versions.

Put the chicken mince, pancetta, spring onions, garlic, chilli, Parmesan and thyme into a bowl. Add plenty of salt and pepper and mix well. Using your hands, shape the mixture into 24 small, firm balls.

Heat the oil in a large saucepan, add the meatballs and cook for about 5 minutes, turning them frequently until browned all over. Add the wine and simmer vigorously for 1–2 minutes.

Add the tomatoes, breaking them up with a wooden spoon. Stir in the sugar, and add salt and pepper to taste. Bring to the boil, then simmer very gently, uncovered, for 30 minutes until the sauce is rich and thickened.

Add the meatballs and sauce to the freshly cooked pasta, toss well to mix, then divide between 4 bowls. Serve topped with extra Parmesan.

parma ham, rocket and bubbling blue cheese sauce

Parma ham crisps up beautifully in a non-stick frying pan and adds crunch to this impressive-looking and sustaining dish. You could also experiment with other cured hams, such as serrano, San Daniele or speck.

- 2 tablespoons olive oil
- 8 slices Parma ham
- 250 g cherry tomatoes
- 2 Bresse Blue or mini Cambazola cheeses, 150 g each
- 2 tablespoons Marsala or sherry
- 2 tablespoons chopped fresh flat leaf parsley
- 300 g pasta, such as pappardelle or lasagnette, freshly cooked
- a handful of rocket
- sea salt and freshly ground black pepper

serves 4

Heat a little of the oil in a non-stick frying pan, add the Parma ham and cook in batches for 1 minute on each side until crisp. Remove and drain on kitchen paper. Add the remaining oil to the pan. When hot, add the cherry tomatoes and cook for 3–4 minutes until split and softened.

Meanwhile, cut each cheese in half crossways, put cut side up under a preheated grill and cook for 2–3 minutes until golden and bubbling.

Break the Parma ham into pieces and add to the tomato pan. Add the Marsala, parsley and salt and pepper to taste.

Add the Parma ham and tomato mixture to the freshly cooked pasta and toss gently to mix. Divide between 4 bowls or plates and scatter over the rocket. Using a spatula, slide a bubbling cheese half on top of each. Sprinkle with freshly ground black pepper and serve.

oven-roasted spicy macaroni

250 g cherry tomatoes

1 red onion, finely chopped

2 garlic cloves, finely chopped

2 tablespoons olive oil

300 g small macaroni

4 boneless, skinless chicken thighs, quartered crossways

200 g chorizo sausage, thickly sliced

2 teaspoons chopped fresh rosemary

1 litre chicken stock

a pinch of saffron threads

8 large uncooked prawns

sea salt and freshly ground black pepper

a heavy roasting tin

serves 4

Inspired by paella, this chicken and chorizo dish is absolutely delicious, and never fails to impress and delight. It's all cooked in the oven, so really couldn't be easier.

Preheat the oven to 220°C (400°F) Gas 7.

Put the cherry tomatoes in the roasting tin and sprinkle with the red onion, garlic and olive oil. Roast in the preheated oven for 20 minutes until the tomatoes are soft.

Remove from the oven and add the macaroni, chicken, chorizo, rosemary, stock, saffron, salt and pepper. Mix well and return to the oven to bake for 30 minutes.

Add the prawns and bake for a further 5 minutes until the pasta and chicken are thoroughly cooked.

parsley and pancetta cannelloni

600 ml tomato passata
150 ml red wine
1 teaspoon brown sugar
1 garlic clove, crushed
1 bay leaf
1 tablespoon olive oil
12 dried cannelloni tubes
150 g mozzarella cheese, cubed
sea salt and freshly ground black pepper

PARSLEY AND PANCETTA FILLING
2 tablespoons olive oil
1 onion, finely chopped
2 garlic cloves, finely chopped
125 g pancetta, cubed
4 tablespoons chopped fresh flat leaf parsley
200 g fresh white breadcrumbs
150 ml double cream
grated zest and freshly squeezed juice of 1 unwaxed lemon

a baking dish, about 30 x 20 cm

serves 4

Don't precook the cannelloni tubes, as it makes them difficult to stuff. To compensate for the moisture they will absorb as they cook, the sauce should be runny – it will become thickened and rich as it bakes in the oven.

Preheat the oven to 190°C (375°F) Gas 5.

Put the passata, wine, sugar, garlic, bay leaf and olive oil in a saucepan. Add salt and pepper to taste and bring to the boil. Cover with a lid and simmer for 15 minutes.

To make the filling, heat 1 tablespoon of the oil in a saucepan, add the onion, garlic and pancetta and cook for 4–5 minutes until softened and golden. Add the parsley, breadcrumbs, cream, lemon zest and juice, and salt and pepper to taste.

Spoon the filling mixture into the cannelloni tubes and arrange the stuffed tubes in the baking dish. Pour the tomato sauce over the top and sprinkle with the mozzarella. Bake in the preheated oven for 40 minutes, or until the top is bubbling and golden and the pasta is cooked through.

pork and parmesan ravioli

Pork and cheese are not a common pairing, but they make a good match if full-bodied flavours such as garlic and sun-dried tomatoes are included in the mix. The filling can be made in advance and kept covered and refrigerated for up to a day.

- 1 garlic clove, chopped
- 1 red chilli, deseeded and finely chopped
- 4 sun-dried tomatoes in oil, drained and coarsely chopped
- 500 g pork mince
- 1 teaspoon fresh thyme leaves
- 4 tablespoons freshly grated Parmesan cheese, plus extra to serve
- 1 quantity Fresh Pasta, rolled into 4 sheets (page 10)
- 1 quantity Tomato Sauce with Double Basil (page 16), warmed
- sea salt and freshly ground black pepper
- a handful of fresh basil leaves, to serve

serves 4

Put the garlic, chilli and sun-dried tomatoes in a food processor and process until finely chopped. Add the pork, thyme, Parmesan, and salt and pepper, then process again until evenly blended.

Put a sheet of rolled pasta onto a lightly floured surface. Put 10 tablespoons of the pork mixture in evenly spaced mounds on the dough, leaving about 4 cm between each mound. Cover with a second sheet of rolled pasta dough and, using your fingers, press firmly round the mounds to seal, expelling any air.

Using a knife, cut lines between the mounds to make separate squares, about 8 cm each. Repeat with the remaining pasta and filling to make 20 ravioli squares in total.

Bring a large saucepan of water to the boil. Add a good pinch of salt, then the ravioli, and cook gently for 6–8 minutes until they rise to the surface and are cooked through. Drain carefully and return to the warm pan. Add the warm tomato sauce and stir to coat. Divide between 4 bowls or plates, sprinkle with basil, black pepper and Parmesan, then serve.

Truffle oil's earthy flavour goes beautifully with mushrooms and makes a great finishing touch to these mezzalune. If you don't have any, use olive oil. To make the soft Taleggio easier to slice thinly, put it in the freezer for 10–15 minutes before slicing.

ham and mushroom mezzalune

2 tablespoons olive oil

1 garlic clove, finely chopped

250 g small chestnut or field mushrooms, sliced

2 tablespoons Marsala or medium sherry

1 quantity Fresh Pasta, rolled into 4 sheets (page 10)

200 g Taleggio cheese, thinly cut into 12 slices

6 slices Parma ham, halved

sea salt and freshly ground black pepper

TO SERVE

truffle oil or olive oil

basil leaves

a round bowl, about 14 cm diameter

serves 4

Heat the oil in a frying pan, add the garlic and cook for 1 minute. Add the mushrooms and salt and pepper to taste and cook for 3–4 minutes until golden. Add the Marsala, remove from the heat and let cool.

Put a rolled pasta sheet onto a lightly floured surface. Put the bowl, upside down, on top of the pasta and cut round it with a knife. Repeat to make 12 rounds from the 4 pasta sheets. Put a slice of Taleggio on one side of each round, add a spoonful of mushrooms and top with a piece of Parma ham, folded to fit if necessary. Dampen the edges lightly with water and fold each circle over to form a semicircle, pressing the edges together firmly to enclose the filling and seal.

Bring a large saucepan of water to the boil. Add a good pinch of salt, then half the mezzalune. Cook for 3–4 minutes until they rise to the surface and are cooked through. Drain carefully and keep them warm while you cook the remaining mezzalune. Divide between 4 plates, sprinkle with truffle or olive oil, basil leaves and black pepper, then serve.

Note If you are not cooking the mezzalune immediately, arrange them in a single layer on a tray lined with greaseproof paper, cover with another sheet of greaseproof paper and chill for up to 2 hours.

SOUPS

pasta e fagioli

2 tablespoons olive oil
1 small onion, finely chopped
2 garlic cloves, finely chopped
1 potato, diced
2 ripe tomatoes, coarsely chopped
1.25 litres chicken or vegetable stock
a sprig of fresh thyme, sage or rosemary
800 g canned cannellini beans, drained
150 g small dried pasta shapes, such as orecchiette
a pinch of crushed dried chillies
sea salt and freshly ground black pepper
freshly grated Parmesan cheese, to serve

serves 4

This hearty soup of pasta and beans is a classic from the region of Puglia in Italy – the pasta shapes traditionally used are *orecchiette*, meaning 'little ears'.

Heat the oil in a large saucepan, add the onion, garlic and potato and cook for 3–4 minutes until golden. Add the tomatoes and cook for a further 2–3 minutes until softened.

Add the stock, herbs, beans, pasta, dried chillies, and salt and pepper. Bring to the boil, then simmer for about 10 minutes, until the pasta and potatoes are cooked.

Ladle into 4 bowls and serve sprinkled with a little freshly grated Parmesan cheese.

summer minestrone

1 tablespoon olive oil

1 red onion, chopped

1 garlic clove, finely chopped

2 celery stalks, thinly sliced

150 g baby carrots, thinly sliced

2 plum tomatoes, coarsely chopped

1.25 litres vegetable stock

150 g runner beans, thinly sliced

50 g small pasta shapes, such as anellini or fedelini, freshly cooked

2 tablespoons Pesto Genovese (page 27), or ready-made pesto sauce

sea salt and freshly ground black pepper

1 tablespoon freshly grated Parmesan cheese, to serve

serves 4

A very light, fragrant version of a soup that can sometimes be rather heavy. It has added sparkle thanks to the last-minute addition of fresh pesto.

Heat the oil in a large saucepan, add the onion and garlic and cook gently for 3 minutes. Add the celery and carrots and cook for a further 2 minutes. Add the tomatoes and cook for 2 minutes.

Add the stock and beans, bring to the boil, then simmer for 5–10 minutes, until the vegetables are cooked and tender. Add the freshly cooked pasta, stir in the pesto and add salt and pepper to taste. Divide between 4 bowls, sprinkle with Parmesan and serve.

conchigliette soup with peas, artichokes and chilli

- 1 tablespoon olive oil
- 1 onion, finely chopped
- 2 garlic cloves, finely chopped
- 2 red chillies, thinly sliced into rings
- 4 slices smoked streaky bacon, finely chopped
- 1 teaspoon fresh marjoram or oregano
- 400 g canned artichoke hearts in water, drained and quartered
- 100 g frozen peas
- 1.25 litres chicken stock
- 75 g pasta shapes, such as conchigliette or gnocchetti, freshly cooked
- sea salt and freshly ground black pepper
- 2 tablespoons freshly grated Parmesan cheese, to serve

serves 4

An incredibly speedy soup that has a wonderful, fresh flavour, yet is made almost entirely from storecupboard ingredients. Enjoy a taste of summer all year round.

Heat the oil in a large saucepan, add the onion, garlic, chilli and bacon and cook for 4–5 minutes until golden.

Add the marjoram, artichokes and peas and stir-fry for 2 minutes. Add the stock, bring to the boil, then simmer for 10 minutes. Add salt and pepper to taste.

Add the freshly cooked pasta to the soup. Divide between 4 bowls, sprinkle with Parmesan, then serve.

index

credits

recipes by Silvana Franco

10, 16–17, 24–25, 28–29, 32–35, 54–65, 78–89, 104–117, 120–125

recipes by Lindy Wildsmith

14–15, 18–23, 26–27, 30–31, 38–53, 68–77, 92–103

photography by

William Lingwood
pages 2, 4–5, 17, 25, 29, 33, 34–35, 54, 56–57, 58, 61, 62, 64–65, 78–79, 80, 83, 84, 86–87, 88, 104–105, 107, 108, 110–111, 112, 114–115, 116, 120–121, 123, 124–125, 126

Nicki Dowey
8, 12–13 main, 14–15, 18, 20–21, 22, 23, 26, 30, 31, 38–39, 41, 42, 45, 46–47, 49, 50–51, 53, 68–69, 71, 72–73, 75, 76, 92–93, 95, 96, 98–99, 100, 102–103

Peter Cassidy
Pages 11, 13 inset, 16, 27, 37 inset, 39 inset, 67 inset, 74, 81, 90–91, 109

Martin Brigdale
Pages 10, 63, 91 inset, 118–119, 119 inset

Ian Wallace
Pages 1, 36–37, 101

David Munns
Pages 66–67, 114 inset

William Reavell
Pages 3, 56 inset

Debi Treloar
Pages 6, 85

Jeremy Hopley
Page 32

Caroline Hughes
Page 59